Psilocybin
Mushrooms

THE GUIDE TO CULTIVATION, SAFE USE AND
MAGIC EFFECTS OF PSYCHEDELIC MUSHROOMS

KERRY
MCKENNA

TABLE OF CONTENTS

INTRODUCTION

In nature there are several types of mushrooms, many of them edible, such as shiitake, shimeji, etc. On the other hand, there are poisonous ones as well as those with hallucinogenic properties and these are also known as psychedelic mushrooms or magic mushrooms.

There are over 180 hallucinogenic species of mushrooms on Earth. Both produce varying amounts of psilocin and psilocybin, which creates an LSD-like psychedelic experience. Four main genera of hallucinogenic mushrooms will be discussed in this series: Amanita, Capelandia, Psilocibe and Panaeolus. Although the best known is the

Amanita mushroom, only Psilocibe and Panaeolus are present in most countries.

Hallucinogenic mushrooms are sometimes labeled psychotropic mushrooms. Psychotropics are chemicals that work on our body's central nervous system and ultimately change our perception, mood, actions and consciousness. In their cultural activities and as recreational drugs, these varieties of mushrooms have been and are still being used by different peoples. In the ancient world there are many accounts of its use.

Mushrooms are usually eaten raw, dried, cooked or used to make mushroom tea (hallucinogenic tea). Psilocybin, found in most magic mushrooms, is the key causative agent of these illusions of reality. This drug binds to the human body's serotonin receptors, which are responsible for controlling other hormones such as sleep, mood, temperature, and appetite. There is no evidence, unlike other medications, that psilocybin can cause chemical dependency.

But this material is not contained in all kind of the mushrooms. The genus Amanita muscaria, for instance, is a psychoactive mushroom, but not a psilocybin. That does not mean, however, that caution should not be taken. Many fungi, such as amanita, are extremely dangerous and can lead to death.

This fungus accounts for 90% of fatal fungal poisoning cases. Long-term use can lead to weakness of the mind.

However, excessive doses can result in seizures, coma, and cardiac arrest.

The main reason why hallucinogenic mushrooms are used is because their effects lead to an inexistent reality for the user. The user may feel stimulated by it in ways they are not used to or feel things that are not actually happening, but are only hallucinations.

CHAPTER 1

Hallucinogenic (psilocybin) mushrooms

Hallucinogenic mushrooms are all mushrooms that contain hallucinogenic substances. Wgen eaten, a person or animal becomes consciousness, introducing itself into a state known as psychedelia or a trip. In the past, such mushrooms were successfully used in religious ceremonies, causing strong feelings. However, the uncontrolled intake of such mushrooms causes irreversible changes in the psyche and to a person's physical health.

Hallucinogenic mushrooms are also called psilocybin since they include psilocybin and psilocin. Psilocybin mushrooms cause a syndrome resembling schizophrenia, which manifests itself after 15 minutes, and when ingested with food - after 2 hours. Usually, those who take such mushrooms complain of tremors, delirium, euphoria, paranoia, and they become restless. There is a distortion of visual, auditory, which is a temporary perception.

Often poisoning causes attacks of aggression, even to oneself, up to when they faint. With poisoning the pupils are dilated, palpitations are rapid, and body temperature is elevated. Changes also occur in the nervous system, manifesting a violation of speech and coordination. Oddly enough, hallucinogenic mushrooms can also cause addiction and withdrawal.

History of Hallucinogenic (Psilocybin) Mushrooms

For thousands of years, hallucinogenic mushrooms, also known as magic mushrooms, have been part of our global culture. These organisms were already circulating on our planet long before they appeared in Woodstock, containing psilocybin. Some people have described the hallucinogenic mushrooms as a legitimate method for exploring the inner workings of the human mind.

The Magical Mushrooms In The Course Of History

These mushrooms have been found in Central America's ancient caves. The use of magic mushrooms goes back thousands of years. The first cave paintings that show the use of this species date back to five thousand years ago. On all continents, from North Africa to South America, we find studies and evidence on the link between humans and hallucinogenic mushrooms.

The first drawings that represent such organisms date back to about 1,000 years ago. Although there has been a lot of speculation about their use, they are believed to have played an important role in religious rituals. These tribes used mushrooms and other psychedelic plants to reach what has been defined as "the flowered dream."

The mushrooms began to spread in Europe after these first findings. In some documents, Cortez documented the use by the Aztecs of mushrooms and other psychedelics. Called "Teonanacatl" by these tribes, which literally means "The God Fungus," these powerful organisms were consumed primarily at meetings and parties by the wealthier classes of Aztec society.

Their consumption was destined for the more affluent social classes at the time as they were expensive and hard to find. The data in our possession is rather scant, but these mushrooms have been used in religious rituals of different religions according to some writings of the 1800s.

In the mid-1950s, psychedelic mushrooms entered the Western culture. It was a scientist of mycology, R. Gordon Wasson, who brought hallucinogenic mushrooms back into the consciousness of the public. It was he who made some trips to Mexico, where he had the opportunity to attend a Mazatec shaman-led ceremony. In a 1957 Time Magazine article entitled "In Search of Hallucinogenic Mushrooms," his experience is reported.

This name was coined by Wasson himself, and is still used to indicate these particular organisms today. A few years later, psilocybin and psilocin contained in mushrooms were isolated by Dr. Albert Hoffman. You may already have heard of him as the first person to have synthesized LSD.

Another pioneer of the psychedelic world, Dr. Timothy Leary, conducted some studies with psychedelic mushrooms, between 1960 and 1962. At that time, psilocybin was still legal, and its use for recreational purposes was spreading, as well as for some laboratory research. Unfortunately, Dr. Leary's colleges did not share the efforts and programs on psilocybin, and his studies at Harvard were quickly interrupted.

However, Leary continued to represent one of the most prominent figures among the promoters of magic mushrooms and psilocybin. Despite their being banned in 1965, hallucinogenic mushrooms and psychedelic experiences defined the decade of the 1960s.

The Prohibition

The 1965 Drug Abuse Control Amendments law prohibited the use of psilocybin and magic mushrooms. The threat of mass hallucinations and having societies in the grip of psychedelic effects frightened people to the point of prohibiting their use. Due to the overwhelming American power, the United Nations quickly followed suit and in 1971 demanded that all members ban psilocybin.

But what are the real reasons for the prohibition of hallucinogenic mushrooms? Were governments really afraid that society might go crazy under their effects, or were they simply afraid these bodies could generate independent thought? Today, there are some countries, including Portugal and the Netherlands, which have decriminalized personal consumption of magic mushrooms.

The Most Recent Progress Made With Psylocibin

Psilocybin is allowed for research purposes despite the general ban. Luckily, the experiments carried out so far indicate that anxiety and other crippling psychological conditions could be effectively treated by these species. Researchers have yet to find out the real reasons for their potential benefits. Those of you who have already used such drugs are going to agree with us that psilocybin has the ability to change the mind, disassociate emotions, and cause intense introspective reflection.

Nevertheless, psilocybin (metabolized into psilocin once it enters the body) is believed to be able to truly open up alternate neural pathways and forge new ones. Such new connections are capable of affecting feelings, allowing people to feel "more connected to the planet." It has also been shown that the symptoms of depression tend to disappear after their treatment and don't reappear for long periods of time.

CHAPTER 2

Growing mushrooms at home - how to grow edible mushrooms at home

Mushroom cultivation today is one of the profitable enterprises that can bring a significant income to the owner at the beginning of his work. Below you can find a catalog of mushrooms suitable for growing. It is worth noting that a lot depends on the professionalism of the workers and the quality of the primary raw material - mycelium. If we are talking about the usual needs of the family, then do not worry at all. Most of the work for you will be done by Mother Nature since the cost of growing mushrooms at home is minimal.

But no matter how many items you want to get, whether you are selling or just want to feast on mushrooms grown with your own hands, the same question arises: how can you grow mushrooms properly? You first have to determine what mushrooms you're going to grow to answer this question.

Statistics show that champignons, shiitake, and oyster mushrooms are easy to grow. And if you take into account that they do not require special care, then a beginner can safely begin to grow them. Nevertheless, some investments will have to be made. An important role is played by the quality of grain or liquid mycelium.

Mushroom mycelium (spores) can be prepared independently, but it is better to spend money and buy a ready-made mycelium from trusted suppliers. The fact is that if the seed is infected with spores of pests or bacteria, there is no reason to hope for a crop.

Another important component is the quality of the substrate or compost. You can also mix it yourself, but you can buy ready-made, which comes in sterile conditions. It is made based on sawdust or pieces of trees with which your chosen mushrooms can form mycorrhiza - fungus root. Such a connection plays a huge role for the fungus, since mycorrhiza provides nutrition to the fruiting body of the fungus, carrying the necessary substances for its growth.

It is the quality of such a symbiosis on which the ability to bear mushrooms will depend. As a partner for growing shiitake mushrooms, it is best to choose substrates containing oak sawdust. For growing oyster mushrooms, birch, alder, and willow stubs are suitable. Champignons will feel great in the presence of sawdust from deciduous trees.

Another point that needs to be considered before growing mushrooms on an industrial scale is the selection of a suitable room. Well, if it is in close proximity to a farm, as it will be easier to satisfy the need for hummus. It can be an above ground or underground structure. It is necessary to avoid the choice of wooden structures since those are at risk of destruction.

Inside the wall must be treated with lime mortar. If you are going to grow and sell mushrooms throughout the year, then you need to make sure that the temperature conditions and optimal humidity indicators in the fruiting chambers are maintained at a constant level.

Additionally, you will need to purchase fans and heaters. It is also necessary to provide for an irrigation system since mushrooms during development and growth will require up to 95% humidity in the room. An important point during the incubation period is the presence of an additional light source. This is especially true for rooms located underground.

However, when growing oyster mushrooms, the lack of good light will not affect its productivity, but it is very dependent on the absence of drafts during the incubation period. In rooms intended for the direct cultivation of mushrooms, it is usually required to install forced ventilation, making sure that the air temperature in the fruiting and incubation chambers does not exceed 20 ° C.

Mushroom Cultivation (Method of Growing Mushrooms)

1. Growing porcini mushrooms

Growing porcini mushrooms on an industrial scale is unprofitable. Therefore, amateur gardeners are often involved in the cultivation of cep. The reason for such unproductive breeding is based on a difficult symbiosis with trees. Strong connections with the root system of trees create ideal conditions for the good growth of mycorrhiza (beekorn). Therefore, for those wishing to engage in the cultivation of ceps, it is necessary to recreate an environment similar to natural conditions. Garden plots on which deciduous (coniferous) trees grow will do just fine with this task. You can use areas in young groves and plantings (5 - 10-year-old), consisting of oaks, pines, spruces, birches. For sowing, a ripe mushroom fruit is needed.

Porcini mushroom, the cultivation of which begins with the selection of an unshaded, moderately moist place, should be planted under the guise of a tree from which the mother process was taken. Look for the absence of nearby herbs such as hoofed grass and ferns.

Sowing preparation.

Several methods for preparing seeds are known. One of them is to grow white mushrooms with mother hats. Hats (at the break the flesh are colored a little greenish) with ripened spores are collected from under the types of trees where planting is planned.

Before planting, they are soaked in a bucket with a solution of weakly diluted manganese (1 g. Potassium permanganate per bucket of water, preferably rain). A bucket will hold about 10-15 pieces, the diameter of which has reached 10-20 cm. Several pieces of sugar (up to 15 pieces) must be added to the water to create a nutrient medium.

The hats must be kneaded, thus contributing to the ingress of ripened spores into the aqueous solution. It should result in a homogeneous mass. Composing infuses takes from an hour to a day. In the preparation of seed, you can use worms and dried hats.

Sowing

Method number 1

Sowing should be done about a meter from the selected trees. Before laying the seeds, it is necessary to remove the upper soil layer (about 15 cm), making sure that the roots of the tree are not damaged. This must be done since the white fungus belongs to the mycorrhiza forming fungi, which grows together with the root system of the tree, forming strong bonds (symbiosis). However, it would be nice if the roots were slightly exposed.

Next, pour seeds onto the roots (350 gr. Per 25 sq. Cm). Top off with removed, loosened soil, and abundantly water it (about 5 buckets under one tree). If the soil at the landing sites is usually wet, watering is carried out only with planting. If dry, then periodically it has to be watered, but not abundantly, preferably by spraying the soil.

Humidification must be done carefully so as not to wash away the inherent mycelium of the cep. It is better to pour water onto a tree trunk. Planting of mushroom spores and watering are carried out in late summer, in the extreme - in early autumn (after the second half of August to mid-September).

Method number 2.

There is another way to grow porcini mushrooms. A small foundation pit is excavated on a shaded area with trees (depth about 30 cm, width up to 2 m). It is necessary to fill it with a nutritious mixture. It is harvested a month before the planned planting of mushroom spores. The composition of the mixture includes fallen oak leaves, which were collected in the spring, 5% rotted oak wood, 5% pure (preferably horse) manure. The leaves are laid in layers of

20 cm, alternating with wood and manure. After forming a pile, pour in 1% ammonium nitrate solution. After a week – use a one and a half mixture warmed up to 36-40 °, and shovel in until it beomes a homogeneous mass.

This mixture is laid in a dug pit with layers of up to 12 cm, with each layer, you pour in a small (up to 10 cm) layer of earth. The total thickness should eventually be about half a meter. In the middle, the bed should have a slight elevation in order to prevent waterlogging of the soil. Planting, in this case, is done with small fragments of mycelium placed in the staggered pits. The distance between them should not be less than 30 cm.

Harvesting

During the summer, it is necessary to monitor soil moisture, especially in arid areas. Watering is carried out approximately once a week with five to six buckets of water, pouring them onto a tree trunk. The fruiting bodies of the porcini mushroom appear in late summer. Productivity is up to 250 kg/ha per season. During the season, you can collect a total of up to a bucket of mushrooms from one tree. There is a lot of evidence of the successful cultivation of ceps at home, in personal plots. By making an effort, and showing patience and care, you can hope that you will have buyers who want to buy porcini mushrooms.

2. How to grow Kombucha

You can take a ready-made drink and enjoy a pleasant taste every day. But you can do it yourself by growing Kombucha. How do you grow Kombucha from scratch? The preparation of tea kvass begins with the preparation of the place of "residence" of the tea mushroom. You will need a three-liter glass jar, gauze, sugar, tea solution, and the body of the fungus (mushroom membrane).

Washing and sterilizing the container is recommended. We're planning a strong tea infusion. You need about 5 cups of sugar and 2 cups of tea. Finish it all with a liter of water. Don't add sugar to the mushrooms in any case. It is important to ensure that no bits of undissolved sugar and tea leaves are present in the tea in the container. The tea leaves must be allowed to cool as this approach will include a living community. Using boiled water for brewing is safer.

If this is a young shoot, you must first add the mother's solution. Pour the tea solution into the jar, then carefully place the Kombucha into it. Cover with gauze and fix it. It must be kept in a warm place, without drafts, and without any direct sunlight. The temperature should not fall below 25 degrees.

The drink is ready in 5-10 days. But at first, it can sink to the bottom. This can last about three days. Then it pops up, as the production of carbon dioxide begins - a product of its vital activity. A ripe mushroom reaches a thickness of several centimeters so that the infusion can be consumed every day, making up for the lack of fluid. It is better to have two containers: one for mushroom growth, the other for a drink. After a while, the mother layer appears at the bottom of the fungus's body, which must be removed.

What else does kombucha need? Caring for Kombucha is not complicated if everything is done on time. The mushrooms should be washed periodically in boiled warm water. This must be done with extreme caution every two to three weeks.

The infusion is poured onto it every two to four days in the summer and every five to six days in the winter. If you overexpose the mushrooms, acetic acid begins to adversely affect the body of the fungus, causing burns. Pieces of undissolved sugar, tea residues, or insects that have broken through cheesecloth can also cause burns.

Although tea itself does not have a direct effect on the viability of the fungus, its deficiency inhibits growth, and excess, on the contrary, inhibits it. If the concentration of tea is low, it is difficult for the fungus to synthesize ascorbic acid, which is important for normal life processes.

How do you care for kombucha when the skin begins to turn brown? This is a clear sign that the fungus is dying. It is necessary to separate the affected layer, rinse it, place it in a new solution. Sometimes a mushroom is reborn on its own. It falls to the bottom of the can, and a transparent film separates from it which is called a daughter process. The old mushroom is reused or discarded. It was also noticed that they were able to sit down to put a tea drink from the mushroom in a cup. After a few days, tiny young mushrooms appeared in it.

The popularity of Kombucha is so great that some countries have put mushroom cultivation on an industrial level. Today, ready-made mushroom infusions for kombucha are produced. However, we prefer independent growth of Kombucha. You can, of course, take a small mushroom from friends and start caring for it in anticipation of a miracle.

But it is better to buy kombucha from growers since the maternal process will be of good quality, and that is the key to the long life of the fungus. It is also known that the quality of the finished infusion depends on the environment in which the growth took place. You can buy Kombucha in Moscow through an online service. The mushrooms will be delivered to you in new sterile containers, 1 cm thick, and detailed instructions will be provided for the cultivation and use of Kombucha.

3. Growing truffles at home

Attempts to "domesticate" truffles have been going on for quite some time. However, the most successful truffle cultivation technology is considered to be Australian. It allows you to get up to 4 kg/ha in a year. In the future (after 5 years), up to 20 kg can be collected per hectare. The Australians themselves say that although this method of growing truffles is expensive, given the cost of mushrooms, it pays off. The cultivation of truffles takes place in several stages.

Infection

Oak seedlings (stony, petiolate) and common hazel are suitable for an infection. In order to obtain well-developed mycorrhiza on the roots of plants, it is better not to infect young plants, namely seedlings, and the seedlings are kept for several weeks under sterile conditions in quarantine, to take the root of the mycelium. After successful inoculation, seedlings must be planted in a nursery, which should be in strict quarantine during the first months. The final engraftment of mycorrhiza lasts about a year until the sprouts reach 20 cm in height.

When choosing and preparing a place, it is necessary to take into account several aspects: the soil should have at least 7.5 - 7.9 rN, high content of humus, and also calcium. It must undergo thorough aeration, and must not contain stones. Directly before landing, deep machining is performed.

The soil should not be contaminated with other fungi. At the time of planting and after (2 years), weeds are not allowed. Treatment with conventional herbicides is not suitable; only those containing rapidly decomposing ai are omitted. This is ammonium gluphosinate. Before planting, the soil is not fertilized to prevent the death of the mycelium. The climate should be dry, with an average temperature of 16.5-22 ° C.

Planting seedlings

Planting seedlings is best in spring, without the threat of frost. On one hectare, there should not be more than 500 trees. Therefore, planting is carried out according to a 5x4 m scheme. A little water needs to be poured into each hole, and a seedling should be pushed in tightly and again watered abundantly. The depth of planting is 75 cm.

A layer of mulch is settled near each seedling (upper layer of forest soil with fallen leaves, radius 40 cm.). Protect with plastic wrap. The development area of mycorrhiza on one tree is 20 m2. The proximity of poplar, willow, chestnut, fir, pine, and lime should not be allowed.

You need to feed with NPK fertilizer, adding a small number of micronutrient fertilizers. The main pests of truffles are rabbits and pigs. Their presence on the territory where mushroom cultivation is being done is not allowed. You also need to monitor so you can notice any appearance of weevils and black cockroaches.

Harvest

The edible portion of truffles includes a fruiting body containing spores. Usually, they are located at a depth of 20 cm from the surface of the earth. Sometimes fruiting body's decay, from which their cost can be significantly reduced. About 15% of the crop grows close to the surface; therefore, in order to avoid damage to the fungi, when cracks appear on the soil, it is sprinkled with sand. Harvest indicator - truffle flies. Truffles are dug out with small shovels.

Growing truffles at home is considered quite troublesome and costly. The reason for this is large monetary investments and a rather long period of return. You will have to spend money on plantation planting, care, protection, planting material, and training. It is known that in France, there are special plantations of truffles. And Australian technology is considered the most suitable. You can implement it wherever there are favorable conditions for the growth of oaks. Yields in nature are much lower than yields obtained on special farms.

4. Growing honey mushrooms

Due to their excellent taste, honey agarics are loved by gardeners. Therefore, the cultivation of honey is one today both in industrial areas and at home. Two types of honey mushrooms are mainly used: summer and winter. If for the first type, there is enough wood waste, stumps or branches, or bars, then for the second type special conditions are necessary. You can also grow mushrooms on the windowsill.

Method number 1

Growing on stumps. The advantage of this method is its simplicity and low economic costs. Suitable for the cultivation of honey agarics both on a personal plot, and in gardens, plantings. Deciduous tree stumps are used as a landing site. Infection with fungal spores occurs in the thickness of the stump, for which it is cut (drilled) in several places. It is in these sections that planting material is laid. If you cover the stump, then the first wave of the crop can be collected in the fall. The most favorable time for planting material landing in April-May.

Method number 2

Growing in banks. The advantage of this method is a convenience, as mushrooms can be grown on the windowsill in a city apartment. The mycelium is placed in the prepared mixture (sawdust, bran, husk), the cooking technology is the same as when growing oyster mushrooms. Harvest can be done 10 days after the appearance of mushroom bodies. One 3-liter can give 1-1.5 kg of honey mushrooms.

5. Growing boletus

The cultivation of boletus is made with the help of grain mycelium. The landing site should be shaded. The mycelium bookmark is best done next to the mycorrhiza forming tree species (aspen, oak, birch), but you can try "cooperation" with fruit or other decorative trees. It is important that the age of the trees does not exceed 8 years. A hole is excavated at the site, the area of which can be 2 by 2 meters, and the depth is 30 cm. The landing of the mycelium should begin no earlier than May.

It should be ensured that the mycelium does not overheat upon purchase or delivery. You can try to grow the boletus mycelium yourself. Pay attention to the properties of the soil. Birchbark prefers to grow in sandy soils. And if there are no suitable trees on the site, then the best way is to bring young trees in from the forest. Then the likelihood of mycorrhiza formation increases significantly.

All material used in laying the mycelium should be processed in order to make sure that there are no competing fungi and pathogenic bacteria. The processing of leaves and sawdust is similar to the technology of processing the substrate for oyster mushrooms.

A surface of fallen leaves covers the bottom of the pit. The first layer's thickness is 10 cm. Fixing aspen leaves is best for the litter job. The humus of the forest is poured over this surface. The second layer's thickness is the same. It is easier to use the soil, taken close to the trees where mycorrhiza can be produced by the bolet.

First, you need to pour out the mycelium cereal boletus uniformly. On top of the mycelium, a layer of leaves and sawdust is covered in another layer. It is important to ensure that the first and last layers are made up of the same material.

From the above, it is necessary to fill in the foliage with ordinary earth. The thickness of the mycelium cover should not exceed 10 cm. The last step is to carefully pour an enriched solution (you can use sugar or special additives) over a bed of aspen mushrooms.

Another way to grow boletus is to bury the ground young fruit bodies of the boletus in the pits near the roots of the trees. They have filaments of mycelium, which also increases the likelihood of mycorrhiza formation. Sowing mycelium spores is another way to get a mushroom crop for next year.

For this, a suspension of mature mushrooms is prepared. Mushrooms are ground, added food flour and gelatin, and poured into the wells. If the weather is dry and hot, the mycelium needs additional watering. The first crop can be harvested in 3 months. The second wave of fruiting will come in two weeks. Fruiting of boletus will continue until the end of October. The total length the beds will last is about 5 years with proper care.

CHAPTER 3

How to Detect Different Types of Magic Mushrooms

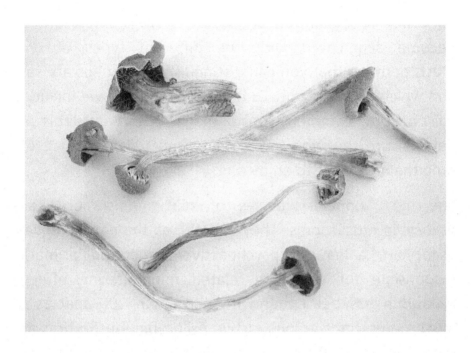

There are hundreds of magic mushroom varieties spread throughout the world. So, whenever you're going to play with these mushrooms, it's important to know exactly how to do it. We will look at the most common kinds of magic mushrooms here. Do not forget to carefully study these varieties and never eat a mushroom without being 100% positive it is non-toxic.

Poisoning of the mushroom is caused by toxins present in some fungi. This happens most often after wild mushrooms have been found to be falsely healthy. The symptoms and severity of fungal poisoning may vary. Although some poisons cause moderate symptoms like gastrointestinal discomfort, others may be fatal.

To order to avoid fungal poisoning, it is important to become acquainted with the different types of wild mushrooms so that you can distinguish which ones are safe and which ones are not. To help you with this, we included a list of some common types of magic mushrooms. This will help ensure that you have a safe and reliable trip every time that you want to enjoy one.

The most popular species of magic mushrooms are psilocybin mushrooms. They contain, as the name implies, psilocybin, a natural psychoactive compound primarily responsible for the fungi-related mind-altering effects. Psilocybin has been found in more than 200 species of mushrooms, but the most active psilocybin mushrooms are those of the Psilocybe genus. Psilocybe mushrooms are growing worldwide, and archeological evidence indicates that they have been used for religious communion, prophecy, and healing by indigenous peoples of Mesoamerica.

Types Of Magic Mushrooms
Do you need help in detecting magic mushrooms? Zamnesia provides an overview of the most common species.

1. Psilocybe semilanceata

Psilocybe semilanceata, also known as a "pointed cone bald head," is believed to be one of the most potent types of psilocybin mushrooms. It is characterized by its large, leather-brown caps and pale, curved stems.

The caps of these mushrooms are 5 to 22 mm in diameter and 6 to 22 mm in size. These can be either conical or bell-shaped; depending on the fungus' hydration, the cap can differ in color. Well hydrogenated caps will have darker brown shades (sometimes with a blue or greenish shade), and grooves may run down them, referring to the lamellae at the bottom. At the bottom of the cap, there will be between 15 and 27 narrow lamellae of Psilocybe semilanceata. These mushrooms quickly turn blue when they get damaged.

Psilocybe semilanceata occurs in both North America and Europe. It tends to grow, especially in meadows and pastures. However, it does not grow directly from dung, like some other species.

2. Psilocybe Cubensis

Cubensis is the most popular type of magic champignon and is usually called a Cuban bald head. It can generally be found throughout the Southeast United States, Central America, South America's northern parts, and in Southeast Asia.

The Cuban bald head has large caps ranging from 20 to 80 mm in diameter. For young mushrooms, the caps may be cone-shaped and appear to flatten with maturity. They have a distinct reddish color that is almost cinnamon-brown. Under the caps, lamellae, which are gray at the beginning and darker with age, are closely spaced by the mushrooms. Mature cubensis psilocybe may have nearly black lamellae.

Generally, these mushrooms flourish just before the year's hottest periods. They have been identified in Cuba for the first time, but are now widely available around the world because they are easy to grow.

3. Psilocybe Mexicana

Psilocybe Mexicana refers to a fungus organism that in Central and South America grows naturally. For thousands of years, these mushrooms have been used by primitive peoples.

In appearance, Psilocybe Mexicana is similar to semilanceata. They have large caps with a cone or bell shape (usually 10 to 20 mm). They may have a small papilla (or umbo) and are generally colored light brown or beige. Such mushrooms may have blue or greenish hues like semilanceata and turn blue quickly when damaged.

Psilocybe Mexicana can grow in groups or individually. It likes shooting from the ground between moss on roadsides and trails, wet meadows or in forest grassy areas. These mushrooms typically occur at higher altitudes between 300 and 500 meters between May and October.

4. Psilocybe Cyanescens

Psilocybe cyanescens is widespread in North America, Western Europe, Central Europe, New Zealand, and parts of the Middle East (like Iran). It is also known as the "Bleeding Bald Eagle." In contrast to semilanceata and Mexicana, these mushrooms have wide, wavy caps that can range between 15 and 50 mm in diameter. The more the mushroom matures, the wavier it appears to be the leaves.

Such mushrooms tend to have a color such as caramel or chestnuts when wet. When they dry out, once completely dried, they become white and wither into bright tawny or slightly yellowish shades. A lot of these mushrooms, including the cap, lamellae, and stalks, tend to turn blue when touched or damaged. Based on the maturity, the louvers under the caps may be light brown or dark purple and appear to have lighter edges.

Cyanescens likes to grow among wood waste, particularly in and along with urban containment of straw-covered plant beds. Indeed, the rapid use of mulch as a form of weed control caused this species to spread to many parts of the world where it had not existed before.

5. Psilocybe azurescens

Psilocybe azurescens, also known as the Handsome Baldhead, is an extremely potent genus of magic mushrooms. Only a small area on the west coast of the United States is known to grow naturally. Although it has been grown around the world in many countries since then.

Azurescens, as its name suggests, appears to have wide, plate-like caps ranging from 30 to 100 mm in diameter. Younger mushrooms may have more cone-shaped caps, flattening with maturity eventually. These mushrooms are usually maroon or caramel-colored when wet and may have dark blue (nearly black) hues when ripe. The caps ' edges might have small grooves coinciding with the slats below. Injured parts of the fungus tend very easily to turn dark blue. There will be dark slats and chalk-white branches on the mature azurescens.

These fungi usually grow in groups on wood waste and / or in sandy soils. They particularly like coastal areas and tend to shoot around dune grasses between September and January.

6. Psilocybe Baeocystis

Psilocybe baeocystis is known as "bottle cap," "knot top," "bluebell," and "olive hat." It usually grows across the Pacific Northwest in the United States. Such mushrooms often have caps of medium size ranging from 15 to 55 mm.

The caps have a cone design and are usually thin and distinctly wavy due to the slats below.

They have a unique color and a dark, olive-brown tone, with steel-blue tints sometimes. The stems are thin, straight or curved and usually appear as chalk-white.

Baeocystis fungi get damahed very easily and then usually turn blue. They love to grow in conifer mulch, wood waste, and / or lawns that are rich in wood pulp. Sometimes they also grow out of the fallen cones of the Douglas fir. They tend to grow in straw-covered garden beds, among other plants such as rhododendrons and rose bushes.

CHAPTER 4

How to Grow Hallucinogenic Mushrooms

The psilocybin mushrooms are a naturally psychoactive living species. They have been used by humans in ceremonial rites and practices for thousands of years.

As their name suggests, these mushrooms belong to the kingdom of mushrooms. Mushrooms are particular organisms. They belong neither to the animal kingdom nor to the vegetable kingdom. Instead, they are forms of life in their own right. However, the DNA of fungi is more similar to that of animals than to that of plants.

What makes the mushrooms so special is their content of a psychotropic substance called psilocybin. Psilocybin is one of the most powerful psychedelic molecules in nature. It is able to manipulate the perception of reality and the behavior of the individual, acting on his central nervous system.

After taking a dose of psilocybin, the subject's perceptions can be distorted or amplified. For example, colors may seem more vivid, sounds may appear deeper, and even the sense of touch may be altered. Psilocybin is also able to condition the emotional and mental state of the subject, creating a state of wonder and veneration. Many people report mystical or religious mental states after taking hallucinogenic mushrooms, as well as long-term beneficial effects on their attitudes towards life.

The substances that the famous anthropologist and psychologist Terence Mckenna called the "food of the gods" have been banned in many parts of the world in recent times. However, some scientists have been granted access to these substances to study their effects on the human brain. The research is still at an early stage and is often prohibited. However, some promising results indicate that psilocybin may have a potential beneficial effect on the treatment and management of many mental disorders.

The hallucinogenic mushrooms grow in various parts of the world at certain times of the year. However, in some countries, the seasons are very short. If you are discovered wandering through the autumn meadows collecting these intriguing mushrooms, you could be prosecuted under the law.

The Essential Rules of Growing Magic Mushrooms

The first and most important principle is: always keep everything dry! Work in sterile conditions so no mold can contaminate the growing atmosphere of your magic mushrooms. -Better wash your appliances and vacuum them twice. Just keep the air as sterile as possible in your office with Bunsen's burner calls.

In any stage of the growing process, make sure something is never opened when it is dusty. You're sweeping up some old books, for example, and some dust still flies into the air. Waiting for the next day is easier.

Never use infected mushrooms; they need a setting that is also a haven for unwanted fungi and many bacteria as well. These are often harmful and can result in severe adverse health effects. Do not worry if anything has been contaminated; it can happen from time to time, and then you must throw away your magic mushrooms. It doesn't matter how much money they cost, the psychedelic mushrooms will grow back really quickly, and the time you've spent is negligible.

The Equipment Needed for Growing Magic Mushrooms

For first-time growers or beginners in general, you should choose an easy-to-grow magic mushroom strain. Not just starting with a Copelandia Cyanescens or similar immediately, they are the strongest hallucinogenic mushrooms, but they are much harder to grow.

Psilocybe cubensis is a good strain for beginners, it has many variants, but it's all classified as easy to develop. You will need:

- A spore or syringe impression of your favorite mushroom, Psilocybe cubensis. - Petri dishes with already prepared agar-agar in which, regularly sold in packs of 5 or 10. So one pack is sufficient.

- A gas bottle Bunsen burner.

- A large and wide needle, a knitting needle will do well.

- 3 or 4 large preservation bottles.

- Several kg rice flour, you better get a big package with 10 kg or more, so you have a stock.

- Several liters vermiculite, too, more is better to have a stock.

- A pan, the most suitable is a pressure cooker. It has to be completely sealed to keep the equipment sterile, and the hot steam would touch each corner.

- 2 or 3 boxes where magic mushrooms will grow. So a big Styrofoam box could be used, or if you build one with some boards, the only important thing is that it can be opened and closed. You must cover all the inner parts of the box with an airtight sheet. The leaf is necessary to ensure your water box and moisture but also keeps the moisture inside your hallucinogenic mushrooms.

- A very sharp knife, the most suitable is a scalpel.

- Organic rye

- Not necessary, but useful, are sterile one-way gloves, surgical masks and when you have long hair, also some surgical headcover.

You can continue with our step-by-step guide to psilocybin mushrooms when you've got everything packed.

Grow Hallucinogenic Mushrooms - Step by Step Guide

Step 1: Plan your developing room and have a non-dusty room where you already have mold problems.

Step 2 : Establish the Bunsen burner and maintain a stable position; it should not fall to the side in any situation.

Step 3 : Get the brush, and Petri dishes and paint in the mushrooms with magic spores. But for now, keep the lids on the Petri dishes. If required, they should be opened and then closed as soon as possible.

Step 4: Place the ready magic mushroom spore paint on your table. Now hold the front of your needle to the flame of the Bunsen burner. Keep it there until it starts to get a little red. Now let it cool again. Now hold it in the flame again, but 3 to 5 seconds will suffice. Wait a few seconds again that is not much more than room temperature and press it for spore printing. Now open the Petri dishes and put the needle tip into the agar and close the Petri dish again. All of this has to be done pretty fast, the Petri dish shouldn't be open more than 3 seconds and it might be right not to take off the lid completely, just lift it and move it a little, so it's only a space of one or two centimeters that is exposed directly to the air.

Step 5: Do this with 3 Petri dishes and place them in a medium temperature in a dark room. Direct sunlight may be incorrect, as the Petri dishes could be badly warmed. Because the Petri dish is a small growth chamber, moisture will not be a concern. You will see how the magic mushrooms begin colonizing through the agar within 4 to 10 days.

Step 6: When the magic mushroom spores have already colonized all over the Petri dish, they are ready for the next step.

Step 7: Prepare a mixture of 1 section of vermiculite and 1 section of rice flour and 3 sections of organic rye. Spread the mixture in amounts that match the containers perfectly. Even if after this phase, you make sure it clean, and try to avoid excessive dust, dirt or bad surroundings such as molded spaces. Attach two small cups of coffee to each bottle before closing the door.

Step 8: Place the preservation vials in the pressure cooker, close it, and place it over low heat. Since preservation vials are made of glass, they could break when heated and cooled too fast. When the pressure cooker is in full heat, leave it there for 60 minutes. Steam is not as hot as your Bunsen burner, so it requires a little more time to make things sterile.

Step 9: Once the vials are sterile, allow them to cool to room temperature, but never open the vial lid. Otherwise, you risk contamination.

Step 10: Take the scalpel and its Petri dishes, which are now colonized with their hallucinogenic mushrooms. Sterilize the scalpel over Bunsen's beak, let cool, now open the lid of the Petri dishes and cut the colonized agar into squares, so that you have around 5 to 10 small colonized pieces.

Step 11: Now put on sterile gloves and perhaps use long tweezers, which are sterile as well. Get the containers, open the lid, and press on and close some colonized agar-agar pieces. Do this as you did by placing the hallucinogenic spore mushrooms on the Petri dishes.

Step 12: Hold the jars in a stable position like you did with the Petri dishes; in a few days' time, you'll see how the magic mushroom colonization scores your food. When you go to the next stage, it's not very necessary to let it colonize until half of the glass is complete.

Step 13: Prepare the same rising media mix that you put in the bottles, add the same amount of water, and place it in the cooker. You should take it out and spread it on the ground of your rising boxes fifteen minutes after maximum heat is achieved. Although susceptible to contamination, psychedelic mushrooms are no longer so fragile.

Step 14: Take the colonized material from a vial and mix it with the media prepared in the grow box. Do this quickly, and DO NOT keep the box open more than necessary.

Step 15: Hold the box at 24 ° C when using Psilocybe cubensis. As the magic mushrooms to grow; check the box for high humidity every day and soak the media with water at all times. Do not spray them with regular water if you see that the moisture does not suit. Regular water in the bathroom often includes unwanted guests, depending on the quality of the water in your region it could even destroy a completely colonized container. Use distilled water.

Step 16: Within a few days, the magic mushrooms will colonize the media throughout the box, and they will start to form the parts of the mushroom you love. If the hat is about to open, harvest it if approximately half of the flush has reached a good length.

Step 17: Bring the magic mushrooms just above the surface and gently twist them so that they almost fall out of themselves, and you don't have to pull violently. When done, spray the box again with water until the media gets wet again. Within 2 days, the next flow will arrive and is ready to harvest within a week. Repeat for a total of four waves. Even if there's more, just set up the freshly prepared grow package, as they're not worth the time.

Grow magic mushrooms with grow kit

Step by step instructions:
Next, see if all the pieces are instantly shipped and ready for use, the cover package, a plastic bag, and a paper clip to close the container, a fork, and warm water.

1. Open the box and take off the lid.

2. Take your fork and stab some holes from the growing kit gently in the ever-increasing press. When you're making two rows of four stabs each, you've got plenty already. They are only needed to ensure that the press can absorb water properly.

3 Slowly fill with warm water, as the media takes some time to absorb it. Fill it until the box is filled with water.

4. Put the cap back on the fully watered grow kit.

5. Let the whole thing sit still for a day.

6. Remove the cap the next day and wash out the extra water.

7. Let the water drip entirely out of the box, and the growing media should have absorbed enough.

8. Fill the plastic bag with 2 or 3 cups of warm water. This ensures proper humidity and will keep the plastic bag large, so it gives enough room for the magic mushrooms to grow.

9. Place the cultivation kit in the water in the plastic bag.

10. Close the plastic bag.

11. Take about 1 to 2 cm from the top of the plastic bag and fold it 2-3 times, now keep it tight and closed with the paperclip.

12 Put the grow kit at its endpoint, to grow, do not move it, as growing psilocybin mushrooms do not like it if they are held around every 2 or 3 days.

13. Fungi don't need direct light, so it doesn't matter where you put your magic mushroom grow kit, but better not put it directly to the sun since it could be a little too hot too.

14. Keep temperatures at 24 to 26 ° C for an ideal magic mushroom growing session,

15. Take a look at your growing kit every day, when you see the first psychedelic mushrooms, keep an eye on the box and media. It must always be moist.

16. Do not open the bag. The magic mushrooms need very high humidity, and if opened every day, they could dry out or slow their growth.

17. Your magic mushrooms should be ready for harvest after a couple of days, and that is the best time is to open the hat. So your magic mushrooms will look a little bit like a lollipop.

18. When harvesting, you have to choose each magic mushroom at a time. Just take it a little above average and set it carefully. The mushroom goes "plop" out of the media; don't just pull them out.

19. Fill the cultivation kit with water again and put the lid on it.

20. This time, you only have to soak it for two hours. The media is still wet and is no longer needed.

21. Replace the water in the plastic bag.

22. Remove the cover from the grow kit and place the box back into the plastic bag.

23. Close the bag and keep it as before, but this time your hallucinogenic mushrooms will appear much faster. The media is colonized, and so there is no delay.

24. Keep checking the box each day. The next day you can see the next flow.

25. Keep continuing this cycle until no more magic mushrooms are growing in the box.

26. By doing everything right, looking at the perfect growing conditions, and with a dash of luck, you can even receive 3-5 waves with your grow kit.

CHAPTER 5

Magic Mushrooms Are the Safest Drug

Psilocybin, the most important intoxicating ingredient in magic mushrooms, has received much attention lately. Not only have studies shown that it may not be as dangerous as it has been depicted in the past. Research even suggests that it may have therapeutic potential for the treatment of depression, anxiety, and addiction. Magic mushrooms could even alleviate the existential fears associated with incurable diseases

Psilocybin - How It Works

Magic mushrooms contain psilocybin, a natural psychedelic alkaloid. When consuming magic mushrooms, psilocybin is broken down into psilocin, which affects the serotonin signaling pathways in two ways: it inhibits the reuptake of serotonin (leading to higher serotonin levels in the brain) and binds directly to the serotonin receptors. This increase in serotonin levels and the activation of certain subtypes of serotonin receptors cause the hallucinations that characterize a fungal trip.

When we talk about a substance's safety, we're basically talking about two things: whether it's addictive and toxic to the body. Psilocybin mushrooms are among the safest drugs available in relation to these two factors.

A report published in 2011 by the journal Regulatory Toxicology and Pharmacology indicated that "the potential for physical and psychological dependence of magic mushrooms is low, acute toxicity is moderate, chronic toxicity is low, and there are negligible public health and criminal aspects."

According to the 2017 Global Drug Survey, psilocybin mushrooms have been the safest of all drugs due to their low toxicity and extremely low addiction risk. A dependence on magic mushrooms can also be created. This dependence, however, is psychological rather than physical.

Another study, conducted by the UK's former drug commissioner, Professor David Nutt, classified drugs for potential harm to the individual and to society. Mushrooms were in the last place. They caused only small self-harm and caused no harm to others. At the top of the most harmful drugs for the consumer and society was - drum roll, please - alcohol.

While animal studies have shown that overdosage with psilocybin can cause death in laboratory animals, so far, this has not been the case in humans. Of the 12,000 participants who took mushrooms in 2016, only 0.2% sought medical help, according to the Global Drug Survey. From a medical perspective, a mushroom trip may not be fatal. But "overdose" can lead to anxiety, vomiting, diarrhea, and a longer and more intense trip.

The biggest risk of taking mushrooms is a "horror trip." It is important to mention that the experience with psychedelic drugs is very subjective. So a bad trip can manifest itself extremely differently. Nonetheless, the effect of a "horror trip" can be enormous.

Unfortunately, there is no way to know in advance how magic mushrooms will work on you. This is especially true at first consumption. However, there are many things you can do to make sure you can enjoy the mushroom experience.

Health Benefits of Magic Mushrooms with Psilocybin

For holistic and health therapy, psilocybin mushrooms may be "the next best thing." There are more than 200 types of mushrooms with psychoactive effects, also known as "magic mushrooms." Such champignons have been used ceremonially in different parts of the world for thousands of years, but only recently, the Western world has discovered its medicinal, health, psychological and emotional effects.

More and more studies are out there that prove that psilocybin mushrooms are far from what the government considers to be addictive and harmful.

Here are some of the most important health benefits that psilocybin mushrooms can offer...

Psilocybin Mushroom Health Benefit # 1 - Stimulates New Brain Cell Growth

A study by the University of South Florida published in 2013 studied the effects of psilocybin mushrooms on fear-conditioned mice.

The main ingredient of psilocybin mushrooms, psilocybin, enabled rats to overcome fear and promoted the growth and regeneration of new neurons in their brains.

After this research, the study leader, Dr. Briony Catlow of the Lieber Brain Development Institute, had some things to say:

"Memory, learning, and the ability to relearn that a stimulus that is already threatening is no longer a danger all depend on the ability of the brain to change its connections. We believe that in psilocybin, neuroplasticity plays a critical role, speeding up the extinction of fear.

In the future, as many interesting questions have arisen from these experiments, it is highly possible that we will continue these studies. The hope is that in clinical trials, we will be able to extend the findings to people.

Psycho-Mushroom Mushroom Health Benefit #2

Reduces discomfort due to social rejection. Sometimes we all go through rejection. When it comes to interacting with other people, it is a natural process.

A study published in April 2016 by a group of Swiss neurobiologists confirmed that psilocybin is a great help in reducing social rejection pain.

Psilocybin Mushroom Health Benefits #3

Relieves OCD Symptoms Obsessive-Compulsive Disorder (also known as Obsessive-Compulsive Disorder) is a psychiatric disorder that exists, especially in patients with depression, bipolar disorders, and other psychiatric conditions.

A study carried out at the University of Arizona in 2006 showed that psilocybin mushrooms are very active in alleviating the effects of this disease.

Psilocybin Mushroom Health Benefit # 4

 Soothes Anxiety - Researchers found in a 2011 study that late-stage cancer patients can alleviate and dramatically reduce their anxiety following psilocybin mushroom therapy.

Psilocybin Mushroom Health Benefit # 5

Reduces Anxiety- Studies have shown that psilocybin mushrooms are active in the very effective treatment of depression as well as post-traumatic stress disorder care.

Psycho-Mushroom Mushroom Health Benefit #6

Long-Term Clinical and Spiritual Benefits - A popular study was conducted at Johns Hopkins University that amazed the researchers.

A third of the 36 guinea pigs said their experience was the most significant (spiritual) of their lives, while more than two-thirds said it was certainly one of the five most meaningful life experiences.

Here's what Johns Hopkins University's Dr. Roland Griffiths has to say about psilocybin mushrooms ' healing power...

"Psilocybin is an amazing tool for unraveling the mysteries of human consciousness. The central feature of this mystical experience is a strong sense of interconnectedness with all things, a growing sense of self-confidence, communal clarity and responsibility, altruism, and social justice. Understanding the nature of these effects and their consequences may well be the key to the survival of the human species. "

Psilocybin Mushroom Health Benefit #7

Connecting the brain in New Ways - Magnetic resonances conducted during the psychedelic experiment caused by psilocybin mushroom micro doses suggest that these 'magic mushrooms' unite different parts of the brain, enabling much smoother interaction between their various parts.

The research has been published in the software of the Royal Society, and the results are very good.

CHAPTER 6

How to Store Magic Mushrooms and Truffles

Successfully growing magic mushrooms and truffles is only half the process, and if you want to keep their effectiveness, you have to store them properly!

There are very few things that are more exciting than the harvest of the first batch of magic mushrooms or truffles. Finally, seeing the fruits of your work creates a satisfying feeling and gives you a much more personal relationship to the substance that will send you on a journey. However, not everything is soft.

Storage of magic mushrooms and truffles can be tricky if you do not know how to do it right. It is very easy to damage them, which reduces potency or makes them susceptible to decomposition. For this reason, it is a must for every aspiring psychonaut to know how to store them safely.

Storage of Fresh Magic Mushrooms and Truffles

The correct storage of fresh magic mushrooms and truffles is actually quite a simple matter. Both can be stored loosely in a dark, cool place, such as a refrigerator, for up to a month. The required temperature is between 2-4 degrees Celsius.

It is best to place the mushrooms and truffles on unbleached kitchen paper. A refrigerator is by nature, a humid place, and excessive moisture can cause damage to the mushrooms. By laying them on paper towels, you are lowering this risk quite a bit.

If a month is not long enough, then you can consider buying a vacuum sealer. Once vacuum-packed and refrigerated, truffles can be stored for up to 3 months.

Dry Magic Mushrooms and Truffles for Long-Term Storage

If a solution is needed for very long-term storage, then magic mushrooms and also truffles can be dried and stored safely in a cool, dark and dry place for up to 2-3 years (maybe even longer). The only risks are insect infestation and potential loss of potency through exposure to light, moisture, and heat. Such long storage is only possible because fungi without moisture content hardly ever decompose.

The trick when drying the magic mushrooms and truffles for storage is to use no heat. It is a common mistake that is often made when trying to speed up the process. However, the active ingredients in the mushrooms can be very sensitive to a prolonged period of heat, destroying them, thereby reducing efficacy.

The process of drying your wizard harvest first begins with pre-drying to remove excess moisture from the mushrooms, followed by a thorough home drying with a desiccant. This will remove any available moisture from them and prepare the mushrooms and truffles for long-term storage.

How to properly dry mushrooms and truffles is explained in more detail in our practical guide. Although it is not about truffles, they can be used in the same way.

Freeze Magic Mushrooms And Truffles

If simple drying is not good enough (though it should), you can go one step further and freeze it. To do this, first, follow our above-mentioned instructions on how to dry them properly. Both truffles and mushrooms must be completely dry before they are frozen. Once dried, simply put in a zip-lock bag and place it in the freezer. Frozen mushrooms and truffles can be stored almost indefinitely.

IMPORTANT: Never freeze fresh mushrooms and truffles; this destroys their internal cell membrane structure, which greatly reduces their potency.

The Effects of Magic Truffles (Psilocybin)

The Magic Truffles contain psilocybin, a psychedelic compound found in hundreds of species of mushrooms and truffles. Its effects cause spiritual experiences comparable to those induced by substances such as LSD, mescaline, and DMT.

A trip with magic truffles can lead to sudden changes in perception, a different conception of space and time, and, of course, hallucinations.

Since truffles and magic mushrooms share the same active ingredient, their effects, whether positive or negative, are almost identical.

Initial Phases

When ingested, psilocybin is metabolized and transformed into psilocin, a molecule capable of acting on the brain's serotonin receptors. The intensity, quality, and duration of its effects depend on the variety of Magic Truffle assumed, the dosage, the physiology of the individual and the surrounding environment.

The first psychedelic effects begin to be felt about 30-60 minutes after ingestion. The entire journey can last from 3 to 6 hours and reaches its peak after repeated psychedelic "waves."

Low Dosage

A small dose of Magic Truffles can cause slight changes in vision, such as increased sensitivity to light and color, greater peripheral vision, dizziness, a strong curiosity, laughter, and strong emotions.

The most sensitive subjects may experience feelings of nausea or cold and nervous attacks. Some people may have visual hallucinations even with low doses of Magic Truffles or other psychedelics.

At Medium Dosages

A medium dose can cause feelings of wonder and admiration. The different perception of time and space is accompanied by hallucinations with open eyes, such as auras around lights, geometric shapes, rainbows, and other colorful and luminous effects.

The ability to concentrate can improve or get worse. The shapes, the objects, the contours, the images can be displayed both with open and closed eyes. The details take on new aesthetic importance, and the things that were normally ignored suddenly take on relevance.

Increased sensitivity generates strong feelings of connection with other people. The artistic vein tends to increase exponentially. At times, feelings of joy can be followed by those of sadness, while any latent psychological problems may manifest during the journey.

At High Dosage

A massive dose of Magic Truffles causes the effects described above, but to the nth degree. Psychedelic hallucinations are lived with overwhelming intensity. Worlds where the psychonaut finds alternative realities. Feelings of wonder, the connection with the surrounding environment, and joy are experienced with extreme impetus. You can also have spiritual or pseudo-religious revelations.

Emotions could touch extremes, and distant memories could suddenly resurface. Abstract entities could take shape in the minds of the psychonauts. These figures can turn out to be both friendly and scary.

Bad Trip and Side Effects

Psilocybin has low toxicity, and the damage it causes is almost irrelevant. However, its effects can be very difficult to manage for beginners or for more sensitive people.

Some people feel tired after a psychedelic journey, feeling chills and cold all over the body, headaches, pupil dilation, nausea, and gastrointestinal disorders.

The first few times, it is advisable to prove the response of your body by ingesting very small doses of Magic Truffles. This is the best way to avoid bad trips.

A bad trip can be such an intense experience that it causes discomfort and panic and fear attacks. Thoughts can start spinning in a vicious circle, and negative feelings can persist for several minutes. A bad trip is a very unpleasant experience, but its duration is temporary, and after a few hours, it completely vanishes.

The best thing to do when experiencing a bad trip is to look for a place to relax, surround yourself with good friends, and never worry about anything. Having a sober and calm person watching over you can be a precious help.

CHAPTER 7

How to Make Spore Footprints Of Hallucinogenic Mushrooms

The Hallucinogenic Mushrooms can be grown quickly in the comfortable walls of the house. However, spores are necessary to do this. Spores can be compared to seeds for plants. So the best way to get spores is to make your own spore magic mushroom prints yourself.

Before going into the discourse on the spore imprints of hallucinogenic mushrooms, we need to analyze some points about the importance of working in a sterile environment. The cultivation of magic mushrooms and the production of spore prints require a sterile environment (or in other words, as clean as possible), as there is a risk of contamination.

Spores or fungi may come into contact with mold or other fungi, which could damage their vitality. Look for a corner of the house where you can work comfortably and clean it in the best possible way. Some argue that the bathroom is the ideal place to start the cultivation process.

In addition to ensuring maximum cleanliness of the surfaces where you will be working, you must also maintain specific personal hygiene. When you enter the area, wear clean clothes, and do not forget to disinfect your hands before starting.

Now that you've cleaned the work surfaces, you'll have to get yourself a couple of things:

- A ripe mushroom with the chapel open
- Asharp knife (preferably scalpel)
- A gas burner
- 2 sheets of clean paper
- A glass
- Tweezers
- A small envelope with zip closure

The spores are located in the lower part of the mushroom chapels, and, consequently, we will have to remove them.

To do this, it is necessary to sterilize the knife by passing the blade over the gas hob until it becomes incandescent. Wait 30 seconds for it to cool and then cut the stem as close as possible to the chapel, avoiding touching the spores.

Take the chapel and place it facing down on the sheet of paper. Spores should not be exposed to air for too long, so cover the chapel with a clean glass. After 2 hours, carefully lift the chapel from the sheet of paper and place it on the other sheet and cover again with the glass.

The spores of the first sheet of paper are more likely to have been contaminated. Those of the second, on the other hand, should be more sterile. This time you have to leave the chapel on the sheet for 24 hours so as to allow the spores to fall.

Remove the chapel from the sheet of paper. Carefully cut the paper around the area with the spores, fold the so obtained imprint on itself, insert it in the bag and close it with sterilized tweezers.

If you want to be even more confident of success, you can wrap the foil scraps. Make sure the sachet is airtight and place it in a dark, cool place. In this way, a spore print can be kept for several years.

Hallucinogenic Mushrooms - How To Work In A Sterile Environment

Depending on the commitment dedicated to their cultivation, the cultivation of hallucinogenic mushrooms can be a more or less simple process. The wide range of products with mycelium that we offer requires only the addition of water!

However, it is necessary to know that the spores of the fungi, the mycelium, and the same fruiting bodies are extremely vulnerable to the contaminating agents. Any external contamination could have catastrophic consequences on the growth of fungi.

This is why it is very important to keep the instruments and the surrounding environment sterile and to take care of one's personal hygiene during maneuvers for the cultivation of mycelium, spores, and fungi.

Spores and substrate can come into contact with contaminants throughout their development cycle. This means that you can never let your guard down, and you will always have to work in a sterile area, maintaining a meticulous and productive cultural attitude.

Here are some tips to help you keep your mushrooms away from potentially harmful bacteria:

1. Wash hands and arms thoroughly with soap and disinfectant. Wear gloves and a mask before starting work.

2. Clean the work area thoroughly with a disinfectant. Always try to use as little space as possible to limit the area to be kept in order.

3. Air contains large amounts of bacteria. Try to perform your cultivation maneuvers in an enclosed area, away from sudden air recirculation that could enter through doors or windows. If necessary, isolate the work area with adhesive tape or similar materials. (Ideally, an incubator or laminar flow hood should be used).

4. Make sure you use a pressure cooker, a lighter, or a blowtorch to perfectly sterilize all the metal tools you are going to use. Remember that if you touch an instrument with your hands, it will no longer be sterile, and you will have to clean it again and disinfect it.

5. Make sure you use a perfectly sterile inoculant. The spores and mycelia are the basis of the whole cultivation

process, and it is essential that they spend the first moments of life in a sterile environment.

6. The substrate may also be at risk of contamination. Its function is to supply nutrients for mycelium and fungi. Inside there are ingredients such as rye, vermiculite, rice flour, and straw, which can contain millions of bacteria. Therefore, do not forget to always sterilize the substrate you will be using with a pressure cooker or a pasteurizing machine.

Hallucinogenic Truffles - How to Consume Them Responsibly

Hallucinogenic truffles are among the safest psychedelic substances to take, but it is still a psychedelic substance that must be consumed responsibly.

The magic truffles can lift the mood, provided that the psychonaut feels competent both physically and mentally at the time of intake. In this way, their effects will be more pleasant and offer even more positive experiences!

An unfriendly environment can negatively affect the journey, while disorder tends to make people nervous, compromising the final experience. So try to find a place where you feel comfortable, perhaps in open spaces.

If this is the first time you are taking a psychedelic substance, make sure you have a person to help you with the hallucinogenic effects nearby.

The best locations for a psychedelic journey are those in the open countryside, far from any external stimulus. Immersing yourself in nature allows you to get more comfortable and positive experiences.

Try to leave a piece of time at the end of the day to regain your strength, rest, and reflect on your experiences. Don't think you will be able to take more consecutive trips, as it is advisable to let at least ten days pass between one "trip" and another.

DO NOT consume hallucinogenic truffles with alcohol or other drugs. Taking truffles with alcoholic beverages can cause anxiety and mental imbalance in unstable people, while the combination with Cannabis or other drugs can intensify the journey and evoke flashbacks.

But above all, try always to maintain a positive attitude throughout the journey, rest assured and enjoy the experience!

CHAPTER 8

How to Identify And Prevent Mushroom Contamination

Growing mushrooms is not a particularly difficult activity. However, it is essential to operate in a sterile and perfectly clean environment.

A single spore of mold can contaminate the substrate, cans, or equipment and can destroy an entire mushroom crop. Read on to find out how contamination occurs, how to detect it, and how to prevent it.

What Are The Signs Of A Mushroom Contamination?

If your mushroom cultivation has been contaminated, usually (but not always) distinctive signs appear. These symptoms differ depending on the type of fungus or bacterium that has contaminated the cultivation.

Slime

Mushroom cultivation can be invaded by different types of bacteria. The mycelium or seed assumes a slimy texture in these situations. This kind of mud grows especially in the areas where the surface is rubbed against the glass. There may also be yellow or brown slime rings around the plant. The colony of bacteria can sometimes develop on the surface of a crust or a gelatinous substance.

Atypical Odors

Not all contaminations must be visible to the naked eye. A strange scent can sometimes mean that something has gone wrong in your mushroom plantation. If the contaminating agent has the same appearance as the mycelium, an unpleasant scent can be helpful in detecting the contamination. Inspect the substratum to detect the scent of moldy, damp, and any smell other than mushrooms.

Discoloration

Luckily, most mold forms have a characteristic pigmentation, making it very easy to spot them. Look for the usual mold colors, which, depending on the type of fungus, can be greenish, blue, red, gray, or black. Keep in mind that exposure does not necessarily cause the discoloration of your hallucinogenic mushrooms.

Fragmentation

If your cultivation of mushrooms is infected with harmful spores, it means that two mushrooms grow simultaneously in your substratum. Since these two mushrooms interact with each other, clear boundaries separating the two mycelia should usually be observed. This is called fragmentation.

And try to identify places where the soil seems to be isolated early from the rest of the plant.

Sporophores

Sporophores are a fungus' small, filamentous structures. Initially, because they are very small, they may not be visible to the naked eye. Many sporophores are larger and can be seen in this situation. The detection of these long vibrissae-like fibers will be simpler with a magnifying glass, with a small "bubble" at the end.

Unusually Smooth And Spongy Mycelium

Some mold forms may make up a very dense mycelium. When you grow it in a bowl, this disgusting fungus will spread rapidly and take up the container's entire volume. In this case, the spongy, smooth appearance of mycelium is very different from the usual mycelium of hallucinogenic mushrooms, and will be easy to notice.

Powdery Consistency

With the naked eye, most forms of fungi can be difficult to detect, but the study can be improved by the magnifying glass. Sporophores of the mushroom frequently form a dusty coating on the mycelium surface. You can clearly distinguish this "fungal powder" from the rest of the substratum with a magnifying glass, and from any benign mycelium discoloration.

Soft White Patches (Overlapping)

The infected area can appear thin, sticky, and crumbly when the surface is contaminated. Such softer areas occur on the mycelium layer and are clearly distinguishable from the rest of the substrate due to their whitish color.

Types Of Contaminating Mushrooms

Penicillin (P. chrysogenum, P. expansum)

Penicillin is the most common type of mold in the world. Penicillin spores spread in the air and can easily contaminate your substrate. The mold then propagates into the can, expanding rapidly to infect the entire mycelium of the mushrooms.

Penicillin contamination is initially white in color and can be difficult to distinguish from the normal mycelium of fungi. Penicillin colonies have a circular shape. Penicillin often develops on wood. Precisely, for this reason, you should never use wooden supports or trays during mushroom cultivation.

Fortunately, Penicillio rarely contaminates the spores to inoculate. In most cases, contamination occurs on grain that has not yet been colonized. Penicillin gives off a smell of mold and dirt.

Aspergillus (A. Flavus, A. Niger, A. Fumigatus, A. Versicolor)

The Aspergillus fungus is another very common fungus that spreads through the air and can infect your cultivation. The Aspergillus mycelium has a light gray color, very similar to the mycelium of hallucinogenic mushrooms. Some Aspergillus species may be yellow, black, green, brown, or blue. There versicolor can take on multiple shades. Sometimes, Aspergillus colonies form a ring, with a thicker layer of mycelium at the edges. Aspergillus has a slimy, musty smell.

Trichoderma (T. Viride, T. harzianum, T. Koningii)

Just like Penicillio and Aspergillus, Trichoderma is a very common contaminating fungus. It is a particularly aggressive species, responsible for the destruction of countless crops. The Trichoderma mycelium takes on a greyish tinge, not always easy to spot. Spores can transfer to the substrate via contaminated soil, dust, or clothing. When the infection is already in place, a dense white layer appears on the surface. Trichoderma spores can produce a yellowish or green mycelium, and the colony is bounded by a whitish ring.

A Trichoderma contamination can occur at any stage of cultivation. Unfortunately, it can be difficult to notice the infection promptly, since sporulation can occur later, after inoculation. This is why mushroom growers should control the odor emanating from the mycelium, to detect the presence of mold and prevent it from spreading. Unfortunately, not all types of Trichoderma fungi have a characteristic odor. Some, however, emit an aroma similar to that of coconut.

Bacillus (B. Subtilis, B. Cereus)

Bacillus is not a fungus, but a type of bacterium. It is, however, a very dangerous and common contaminant in mushroom cultivation. B.subtilis, heat resistant, is the most widespread species. The presence of this bacterium manifests itself with a sort of crust or muddy area on the substrate. Contamination occurs mainly due to inadequately sterilized equipment. The risk of infection is greater when inoculation syringes are stored at higher than environmental temperatures. You can identify the Bacillus contamination thanks to the disgusting smell of rot emitted by this bacterium.

Mucor (Cat Hair)

The "cat's hair" mold is so-called because of its thin filaments (sporophores), with small heads on the ends. It is a contaminating mold that can attack the spores of inoculated fungi, but rarely develops on the substrate.

Rhizopus (R. Stolonifera, R. Oryzae)

Rhizopus is another contaminant. It is a very difficult mold to manage because it can spread very quickly. It has a similar appearance to "cat hair" mold, with long hair-like filaments, with a rounded tip. Rhizopus has an acrid smell, which sometimes resembles that of alcohol.

Fusarium

The Fusarium mycelium can easily be confused with that of hallucinogenic mushrooms because it has the same whitish color and grows at the same speed. The Fusarium, however, develops a brighter and brighter color, which, after a couple of weeks, can become pink, purple, orange or yellow. Often the Fusarium spreads in the mycelium due to inadequate sterilization of the work tools, and it can also contaminate the cans used in the PF technique.

Yeasts

Yeasts are another very common contaminant and, like fungi and bacteria, can destroy an entire crop. The presence of yeasts occurs with small spots inside the vase, usually yellow or white. Some types of yeast may resemble bacterial contamination. Yeasts usually do not attack substrates, but may be present in the spores to be inoculated. Yeasts give off various odors.

How To Avoid Contamination Of Mushrooms

The basic rule is to always operate in a sterilized atmosphere and follow strict hygiene protocols if you want to grow mushrooms successfully, preventing harmful contamination. Only one noxious spore or bacteria is necessary in most cases to contaminate the entire production of mushrooms. Normally, in a 100% sterile environment, such as a laboratory, hobby growers do not function. Nonetheless, several measures are in place to minimize the risk of pollution.

Sterile Cultivation Environment

Some pollutants are released into the atmosphere, such as molds and fungi. They can be anywhere, and you can't see them, even in relatively clean places. It can, therefore, be difficult to remove these toxic molecules. Researchers use specially filtered air cabins called laminar flow hoods in professional laboratories. This particular equipment is, sadly, very costly, and definitely beyond the scope of an occasional mushroom grower. But, if you love DIY, on the other hand, you might be able to build a semi-professional laminar flow hood.

Sterilize Substrate and Wheat

Airborne compounds that contaminate the mushrooms are a major problem. But they are often already present in the soil as well. Most substrates and loose grains contain harmful species that must be extracted or at least reduced prior to use. Before inoculating the spores of the fungus, you must sterilize both the substratum and the seed.

Using a pressure cooker that is large enough to hold all the stuff, you may sterilize sawdust blocks and wheat grains. Place the block of sawdust in the pot and sterilize for about 2 hours and a half. For wheat, it will be enough to do it for 1 hour and a half.

Sterilization is a procedure that removes all types of bacteria. Pasteurization is another method that uses heat to remove most bacteria. Pasteurization is not adequate to sanitize sawdust blocks, but it is a valid technique if you use straw as a substrate. To pasteurize the straw, heat it at 65–82 ° C for at least an hour and a half. Some growers put the straw in a pan full of water, and then heat it up on a stove.

Try To Stay Clean While Working With Mushrooms

We now know the factors that may contaminate the atmosphere, the soil, and the surface. But the main source of pollution we have not yet considered: yourself!

Your clothes, body, and hair can serve as contaminant vectors. Personal hygiene is important to grow mushrooms in the best possible conditions.

Take a shower and wash your hair before you focus on your mushrooms. It's not a short shower we're talking about. Rub the skin well, wash thoroughly in every area of the body, even under the nails and behind the ears. To kill bacteria on the body, hand sanitizing items can be very useful.

In professional laboratories, operators wear a white coat. You probably won't have such a sterilized uniform available, but you should still use clean clothes before you start working on your cultivation. It is advisable to also wear a mask.

Use Sterilized Instruments

Obviously, it makes no sense to work in a perfectly clean environment if sterilized instruments are not used. In other words, you need to sanitize all equipment and tools, such as scalpels, blades, and syringes.

When using the scalpel for transfers, you must remember to sterilize it. To do this, heat it over a flame for about 30 seconds until it turns red. You can use a Bunsen burner or an alcohol lamp. If you have nothing else available, a lighter is also fine.

Clearly, you cannot heat the syringes and plastic instruments over a flame. In this case, you must use alcohol to sterilize them.

Alcohol is also useful for cleaning all surfaces, including cans and bags. A couple of bottles of denatured alcohol (isopropyl) and a few sheets of blotting paper will allow you to keep your workspace clean and disinfected.

CHAPTER 9

The Difference between Psychedelic Mushrooms and Psychedelic Truffles

Perhaps the most popular psychedelic drug in the world is magic mushrooms. Large numbers of people have had the opportunity to experience their influence over the years, using them for the most varied purposes. Psychedelic mushrooms, however, have become illegal in almost every country in the world over the past two centuries. Let's try to understand the distinctions between magic mushrooms and truffles because there are always variations.

What Are Magic Mushrooms?

Magic mushroom is a term used to refer to a class of hallucinogenic properties of more than 180 species of fungi. We contain a significant amount of psilocybin, psilocin, and baeocystin, both compounds which, due to their specific effects, have attracted human interest. Such compounds are already developed in the fungus in the early stages of growth, but they reach their peak concentration and power only during the last stage of development.

It has been recorded that psychedelic mushroom use has been part of human history for more than 3,000 years, during which cultures around the world have used it for the most varied purposes. They may even have contributed to the development of human consciousness, according to some hypotheses, as humans started to include them in their diet.

What Are The Magic Truffles?

Magic truffles are not very different from magic mushrooms. These contain exactly the same psychoactive chemicals as their fungal counterparts, but they are more lightweight and cleaner. Hence, those who say mushrooms are stronger than truffles have most likely used magic truffles that were not fully developed.

Truffles were considered separate species from fungi up to the second half of the 19th century. Since then, we know that mushrooms and truffles in the life cycle of the fungus are nothing more than the expression of a process. But is it special or is it the same thing?

Mushroom Biology

Before revealing the differences between these two organisms, we need to understand the growth process of a fungus.

Under the right conditions, the fungal mycelium appears in the ground and in the compost in the form of a whitish veil similar to mold, which develops above and below the ground. This is how all psychedelic mushrooms are born.

The next process will determine whether the mycelium will become a mushroom or truffle.

If all goes well, the mycelium will allow the development of mushrooms. If, on the other hand, the levels of humidity and oxygen, or the availability of nutrients are not within the optimal values, the fungus will have difficulty growing. When this happens, the mycelium creates an underground sclerazio, also known as a truffle. This is the real difference between these organisms. The truffle is nothing more than a survival technique adopted by the mushroom when it does not have the possibility of growing into a proper mushroom.

But Then What Are The Differences?

There is no real difference between mushrooms and truffles. If you happen to take them separately in capsule form, you would not be able to distinguish the differences between their effects. You can recognize them by their appearance and smell, but not by their effect.

Both cause very similar effects. The only difference is that truffles offer greater uniformity when they are used. Mushrooms increase their potency as they grow, which means that a badly grown mushroom will never be as strong as a properly grown one. Truffles, on the other hand, do not follow this mechanism. Once you have mastered a certain dose, you will be sure that that amount will induce you the same effects, even the subsequent times.

CHAPTER 10

Poisonous mushrooms

Some mushrooms are known to be poisonous; a person receives serious poisoning when these are ingested in ordinary doses. Poisoning is categorized into three classes by the existence of the action of toxins found in poisonous mushrooms: local irritating mushrooms (food poisoning); fungi that cause abnormal function in the central nervous system; and poisoning that leads to death.

Poison mushrooms are particularly dangerous due to the nature of the action on the human body leading to death. The action of toxic substances occurs gradually, without causing noticeable changes. However, with the onset of irreversible reactions in vital organs, a person begins to experience deadly pain. Mortality from poisoning by poisonous mushrooms reaches 90 perent in some cases! Poisonous mushrooms are especially dangerous for a child's body. Therefore, if children go into the forest with you, it is important to ensure that they do not try mushrooms "on the tongue."

The main distinguishing feature of poisonous mushrooms is the presence of deadly substances in them, and not the external similarity or absence of any "normal" mushroom trait. Some dangerous signs are sometimes completely absent in some representatives of poisonous mushrooms.

This applies to cases where, for example, flakes on a fly agaric hat are washed away due to heavy rain.

Death cap

The most toxic among all representatives of the mushroom kingdom is pale grebe. It belongs to the family of fly agaric, the Amanite family. Although poisoning with this fungus is not so common, mortality can still reach 90% in some cases. That is why it is necessary to take a closer look at the pale grebe.

The fruit body of a pale toad cap - In young mushrooms, the body is completely hidden under the film, having an ovoid shape. On the hat at this stage of growth, there are remains of a flaky coverlet. The color of the hat at the beginning of the development is an olive or greenish hue, then the color becomes lighter. Sometimes there are pale toadstools with a completely white hat. The hat can reach 15 cm. As it grows, it flattens, sometimes with the edges turned up to the top. The pulp is white with a pleasant mushroom aroma that does not change color when pressed.

The leg of the pale grebe reaches a height of 15 cm in mature mushrooms, remaining thin (only 1-2 cm). In young mushrooms, it seems thickened. It has a white sack-shaped Volvo, a white strong ring, either erect or hanging. The

Volvo itself is wide, free, cupped, white, often torn, and immersed in the soil. The color of the legs is white, sometimes with beautiful stains in the color of the hat. The plates are frequent, lanceolate, wide, free, and white. The spores are also white.

This type of mushroom is often confused with floats, young forest mushrooms. However, they can be distinguished by the absence of a ring on the leg of a pale toadstool. In young champignons, the plates are pink and then lilac. In a pale toadstool, they always remain white. There is also some similarity with rows and russules. It is possible to determine the edibility of the fungus by the absence of the vulvar ring on the leg. But caution will be dictated by the following principle: it is better to lose the opportunity to taste a dozen floats mushrooms, or russula than die, having tasted only one toadstool.

Pale grebe poisoning is not excessively fatal! The whole problem is that the first signs of poisoning that have entered into force can occur much later than right after eating them. The insidiousness of a pale toadstool is comparable only to the insidiousness of the poison of the gyurza. Penetrating into the human body, toxic substances begin their deadly irreversible destruction 10-30 hours after eating them. It can all start with a normal headache. But subsequently, it turns into impaired vision, burning pains in the stomach, intense thirst, and a restless state.

Then cramps, cholera-like vomiting, and diarrhea join in. Sometimes relief comes (a period of false well-being), but by then, irreversible changes have occurred in the liver, kidneys, heart and spleen. When toxins have already entered the bloodstream (at the onset of symptoms), death usually occurs within 10 days. The lethal effect is so strong that 4 mg is enough for poisoning a cat, poison, for a dog - 25, and for a person - 30 mg.

However, if you suspect a poisonous grebe poisoning and seek help from specialized institutions in the first few hours, the mortality rate decreases to 50%. The poisonous mushroom pale grebe may have its value in the forest ecosystem. However, while not much is known about it, it is better not to put mushrooms in your basket, in which you are 100% not sure.

Fly agaric

Fly agaric belongs to mycorrhizal lamellar hat-leg mushrooms. The very name "fly agaric" came from the use of this fungus as an effective tool in the fight against flies and other insects (bugs, mosquitoes). It is generally accepted that only poisonous mushrooms, causing severe poisoning, belong to the fly agaric family.

However, the fly agaric species have at least 6 representatives, which are good, edible mushrooms. There are also some that are conditionally edible, but with proper preparation, they are quite edible. And only a few, such as Amanita muscaria, Amanita muscaria, Amanita smelly, Amanita panther, and Amanita muscaria are poisonous mushrooms. In total, the genus Amanita has more than 600 species.

The fly agaric hat is fleshy, thick, in some representatives thin, sometimes with a tubercle. The hat is easily separated from the leg. The color of the hat has various colors (red, shades of white, green). The remains of the bedspread, in which the fungus is at the first stage of development, form whitish flakes, shreds that give a characteristic, recognizable appearance of fly agaric.

It is easy to separate, leaving a ring, in some fly agaric mushrooms, the flakes adhered to the cap. The edges of the cap are finely fleshy, smooth, scarred. Amanita mushroom has a large fruiting body (in most representatives), standing on a stalk. In the embryonic state, the first stage of growth is completely enclosed in a coverlet.

The leg of mature mushrooms has a cylindrical shape, a straight line, expanded at the base. Amanita pulp is usually white. Some representatives of fly agaric stain the flesh when cut, emitting a sharp, bad smell. The plates are either weakly grown or loose. Their color varies from white to yellowish. Under the hat, plates of various lengths can be located.

Red fly agaric (description). Refers to poisonous mushrooms that cause severe poisoning, which is sometimes fatal. Some tribes consume Amanita muscaria after special treatment. The active component of muscimol contained in the Amanita muscaria is a powerful hallucinogenic drug, which was previously used as an intoxicant that causes convulsions.

The caps of red fly agaric are usually hemispherical (almost mature in mature mushrooms). The size can reach 20 cm, in young mushrooms - about 8 cm. The color is bright red with white flakes resembling warts. They are always present in young fly agarics, in more mature ones they can be washed off by rains. The skin is shiny.

The edges of the cap of the red fly agaric are slightly rough. The pulp is white. On the cut, the color varies from light yellow to orange. The smell is practically absent. It tastes a bit sweet.

The plates are white (sometimes cream), frequent. There are intermediate plates. The leg is thick, fleshy, reaching a width of 1.2 cm. Mature mushrooms have a hollow leg, the color of which is from white to yellowish. In the upper part of the leg, there is a hanging film ring.

Amanita panther, which is also a poisonous representative of fly agarics, is distinguished by the color of the hat. It is from brown to grayish-olive shades with traditional white flakes.

Satanic mushroom

The satanic mushroom (Satanic boletus) belongs to the genus of boletus. It is really very similar to pink-golden boletus. But unlike the latter, it is a poisonous mushroom. Most often grows on calcareous soil, in close proximity to oak, hornbeam, hazel, and linden in the southern parts of Europe, Asia, and the Middle East.

Satanic tinder reaches a large size at the end of summer, the hat of which by that time could reach 30 cm. In shape, it is rounded and pillow-shaped. Mature representatives have a more open form. The peel on the hat is velvet, sometimes smooth to the touch, dry. Color ranges from white to off-gray and olive. There are specimens with a yellowish, greenish tint. The leg of the satanic mushroom is massive, reaches 15 cm in height and up to 10 cm in thickness.

Young mushrooms stand on a spherical pedicle, changing to barrel-shaped or repetitive as they grow. In mature mushrooms, the leg is dense, with a carmine-red mesh pattern in the middle. Above, it is somewhat narrowed, yellowish red. The flesh on the cut turns slightly blue, but sometimes it turns red. Old, overripe mushrooms have an unpleasant smell of rotting onions.

In its raw form, the satanic mushroom described above is very toxic. However, in some European countries, they treat it as conditionally edible. It has been proven that the high toxicity of the fungus persists even after prolonged cooking. Therefore, even an experienced mushroom picker should remember that the satanic mushroom is a poisonous mushroom!

The satanic mushroom is similar to a beautiful boletus, characterized by yellow tubes. Some similarities are also observed with bitter pain, with the exception of a lighter hat and yellow tubes. The purple fly is similar to satanic, but in the section, it has a dark blue color. The similarity is observed with other representatives of the flying ones: false satanic mushroom, yellow boletus, diabolical mushroom, olive-brown oak, and speckled oak.

Silverfish

This mushroom bears fruit for a rather long period of time - from July to October. It grows mainly in meadows, gardens, pastures, mixed, coniferous and deciduous forests. Young mushrooms have a whitish, with a red tubercle, a convex or flat-convex hat 2-5 cm in diameter. The top of the mushroom cap is covered with brownish-reddish scales.

The fungus has a hollow, slightly thickened, cylindrical pedicle about 0.3-0.8 cm thick and about 4-8 cm long. The plant has rounded triangular spores, the plaques are frequently white. On the leg is a white or pinkish membranous ring, but as soon as the mushroom ripens, it disappears.

The mushroom has a thin and white flesh, it tends to blush on a break or when touched. The pulp has a rather unpleasant taste and a sharp rare smell.

Remember that the mushroom belongs to the category of very poisonous, so it is still forbidden to eat it in any processed form. Externally, silverfish have similarities to the fungus lepota corymbus, which is edible. Therefore, inexperienced pickers can easily confuse these types of mushrooms.

Raincoat

The body of the fungus is 3-5 (12) cm in diameter and 3-6 cm high. The body has an ovoid, tuberous, spherical flattened shape, but the leg is completely absent. The mushroom pulp is light, yellowish-white, but with age, it darkens significantly. It remains dense for a very long time until it decomposes when the mushroom is fully ripe, into olive-brown spore powder and grayish-yellow sterile areas.

This mushroom grows from July to September - early October. The most favorable area for them is on rotten wood in coniferous and deciduous forests, on soil, in fields, and young plantings grow on the side of paths or roads, and on the edges of the forest, and in glades.

Raincoats love pebble and dry sandy soils. They can also often be found among rare grass or in moss. They often grow in groups. By the way, they can easily tolerate even the most protracted drought. In Russia, they are found mainly in the Far East, in the North Caucasus. By external signs, an inexperienced collector may confuse false raincoats with the same mushrooms with scaly or areola peridia and prickly spores.

Note that this mushroom is inedible. In large quantities it is slightly poisonous, and it can cause serious gastrointestinal upsets. There may be an allergy to spores in the form of rhinitis or conjunctivitis. Only a small amount of mushrooms at a young age are allowed to be eaten because they resemble truffles in smell and taste. Despite this, doctors do not recommend consuming these.

Poisoning poisonous

This type of mushroom is very toxic and dangerous to human health. If you use it in food, even in small quantities, it can cause gastrointestinal upset in serious forms. The reason is the unexplored toxin that is contained in these mushrooms. Its danger to a greater extent consists in the fact that it has a very pleasant smell and taste, therefore it is difficult to perceive it as poisonous.

Most often, this mushroom can be seen in deciduous and coniferous forests. Although it is a mycorrhizal fungus, it can also be often found on the forest edges, where they are found in large groups, forming the so-called witch rings. These mushrooms are most fruitful from August to October.

As for the poisonous hat, it is first spherical in shape and then becomes flat-spread with a curled edge. Its color is grayish-white, off-white or blackish-gray with a bluish tint. On top of it is covered with flaky scales, which diverge concentrically. The pulp of the mushroom is very dense, grayish in color with a floury smell.

The mushroom is very poisonous, can cause serious damage to the gastrointestinal tract, therefore, we do not recommend eating it.

Help for Mushroom Poisoning

It happens that inexperienced mushroom pickers often confuse edible mushrooms with poison mushrooms and, of course, use them for food. Mushrooms can also be poisonious if improperly cooked. Therefore, when collecting mushrooms, do not take those that are in doubt. And when you get home, and sort them, make sure you only have edible ones in the basket. We can learn first aid for mushroom poisoning from this post.

Unfortunately, mushroom poisoning is not as rare as we would like it to be. Therefore, you need to learn how to provide first aid for yourself and those near you. And this first aid plays an important role in saving a patient's life.

At about 2 hours, the first signs of poisoning occurs, which is a profuse upright stomach, abdominal pain, nausea attacks, and malaise. So soon as possible, you need to call an ambulance. If the signs of poisoning occur after 6 hours or more, it will be even more serious.

The main feature of mushroom poisoning is that the toxins of the fungus are poorly soluble. In a person exposed to a poisonous fungus, poisoning can occur. And even if the symptoms of fungal poisoning may vary from nutritional poisoning symptoms, all the precautions given to the patient before an ambulance arrives, are the same.

Poisonous mushroom poisoning is divided into several types:

The first type

This type includes some small types of umbrellas and pale beads, and fly agaric. Symptoms of poisoning can occur from 6 to 24 hours and may occur after 48 hours. It begins with urine, thirst, severe diarrhea, vomiting, and convulsions. After 3 hours, there is a time of apparent improvement, jaundice appears, and then the patient dies of impaired liver function.

The second type

These include lines and some species of the Helliwell family. Signs of poisoning appear after 6 or 12 hours, and perhaps after 2 hours. They are expressed as a feeling of fatigue, vomiting, stomach cramps, and a headache, lasting 1 or 2 days. Then comes jaundice and a liver disorder. Sometimes this poisoning leads to death.

The third type

These include fibers and webs. The first signs of poisoning can occur after 3 to 14 days, and sometimes later. There is a feeling of dry mouth, pain in the stomach, increased urination, and vomiting. Then the kidneys stop working and death occurs.

The fourth type

They include some fertilizer. Signs of poisoning appear only if a person has consumed alcohol after eating a fungus, even if 2 days have passed. Thirty minutes after drinking alcohol, flushing of the body and face begins, vomiting, diarrhea, stomach pain, and heart palpitations. This can happen every time you drink alcohol. This poisoning is not fatal.

The fifth type

This group includes the panhomer muhomorah and red, fiber and whiteheads. The first signs of poisoning appear after half an hour, and sometimes after two hours. The face turns red, heart palpitations, sweating, swelling, impaired vision, and a feverish condition without fever.

Sixth type

These include the mense, the mesh and the agaric. The first signs of poisoning appear after 30 minutes, and sometimes after 2 hours. They are expressed in a state reminiscent of the state of alcohol intoxication, agitation, and heart palpitations. After a few hours, everything goes. Poisoning is not fatal.

The seventh type

These include yellow-skin champion, fake gray-yellow chicken, many enolmies and more. The first signs of poisoning appear after half an hour or 2 hours. They are expressed in diarrhea, vomiting, dizziness, colic, headache, and nausea. These poisons rarely end in death.

Eighth type

These include volatile agar porphyry. Poisoning occurs after the consumption of such mushrooms in large quantities.

The ninth type

To this group is the slivite thin. Poisoning can even occur several years after a person has used this pig food. Usually the pain starts in the abdomen, then comes dizziness and it ends with impaired renal function.

Remember these simple rules to avoid mushroom poisoning:

- Collect only known types of mushrooms.
- No need to collect old mushrooms.
- You should not taste mushrooms you do not know.
- When collecting flash, carefully consider the coloring of plates and hats. Do not cut them into bundles, carefully consider each mushroom.
- Do not put mushrooms in bags.
- Do not collect mushrooms near businesses, near roads, or in the city.
- Do not leave mushrooms overnight without treatment.
- Canned mushrooms can cause severe poisoning

CHAPTER 11

How to Grow Hallucinogenic Truffles Alone

Mushrooms are fantastic and fascinating living creatures. They play an essential role in the environment. Their DNA, incredibly, is more similar to that of animals than to plants.

In addition to the list of incredible features that mushrooms possess, the largest organism ever discovered was a mycelium network that stretched for 2,200 acres, under the Malheur National Forest in Oregon.

The most popular mushrooms known to man are various, from those used to make tasty recipes to the opposite extreme where psychotropic varieties are placed.

Specifically, these include mushrooms containing psilocybin or "magic" mushrooms. This genus of mushrooms has been used by man for many generations, to favor psychedelic experiences and exploit the apparently beneficial effects.

However, hallucinogenic mushrooms are not exclusively present in the form of simple mushrooms. Sclerotium, or plural sclerotia, is a structure composed of fungal mycelium.

It stores the nutrients for the fungus, allowing it to survive in harsh environmental conditions. These sturdy parts of the mycelium network allow the fungus to adapt and withstand extreme temperatures, unpleasant humidity levels, and water shortages. A sclerotium is also a part of the life cycle of some fungi and resembles nuts or small stones.

There are many species of hallucinogenic mushrooms on planet Earth. However, only a small part of them possess the ability to form sclerotia. These varieties include Psilocybe tampanensis, Psilocybe pajaritos, Psilocybe mexicana sclerotia, Psilocybe atlantis and Psilocybe hollandia.

The sclerotia of these species, also known as "hallucinogenic truffles," contain the psychoactive substances psilocybin and psilocin, much loved by the psychonauts.

How to Cultivate Truffles

Beginning from scratch is one way to grow truffles. To do this, all the raw materials required to complete the process will need to be identified. Truffles grow in a soil type called a substratum.

A substratum is a layer of materials that are beneficial for truffles to absorb and grow nutrients, a little like the plants growing in the soil. Simple grass seeds are one of the most selected substrates to grow truffles.

- You will first need to choose a container. Mason Jar glass jars are a great choice. Before using them, wash them as perfectly as possible.

- Fill the glass jar with the substrate, up to about half, to make room for growth. Then fill the jar with water and let it sit for 12 hours.
- Then drain the substrate. Now it is time to sterilize the substrate, so as to make it ready for inoculation.
- You can do this by initially creating holes in the lid of the container to allow the pressure to escape. Then put the jar in a pressure cooker for about an hour at 15 psi (pounds per square inch).
- This point is essential for your safety. When sterilizing, make sure you use a Mason jar and not a normal glass jar. This will prevent the jar from exploding. Also, allow pressure to come out of the can, keeping the lid loose and making holes in the lid.
- After the substrate has been sterilized and cooled, shake the material to prevent lumps from forming.
- Now you can proceed to inoculate the substrate. This can be done using a simple spore syringe. After injecting the spores, close with a lid without holes and shake the jar again to distribute the spores evenly.

From now on, the content must be processed for about 2 to 4 weeks in an atmosphere between 21 and 25 degrees Celsius. You can place it in an incubator for convenience.

The mycelium will have colonized the soil after this period of time. It's just a matter of waiting at this point. Regularly check the jar to ensure that the mycelium grows at the desired temperature. You should have fully developed truffles in around 3 or 4 months.

Cultivation Kit

A much simpler and cheaper solution to grow truffles is to buy a ready-to-use cultivation kit. These practical kits contain material that has already been inoculated and colonized. So all you have to do is wait for the truffles to grow and reach full development.

CHAPTER 12

Mushroom drying

Mushrooms can be dried in many respects. We'll talk about the most popular methods in an ordinary apartment that can be used at home, as well as remembering the old drying methods.

Note that it is not possible to dry all mushroom styles. Upon drying, leaf mushrooms generally become bitter. Additionally, this subspecies has exceptions. For example, fall, summer and winter honey mushrooms and deer mushrooms.

"Natural" drying

Natural drying can be called drying in the sun. It is impossible to completely dry the mushrooms in the sun, as they only dry out, but near the end, they will need to be dried in the oven.

Put pre-peeled mushrooms on a tray that can be covered with paper. Never use a baking sheet from the oven, otherwise, your mushrooms will simply "fry."

Choose only warm days for drying, when the sun shines brightly and there is no wind. In this weather, mushrooms will be ready in two days. To determine the readiness of mushrooms, you need to take one and bend it. If it succumbs and bends, then you did everything right. Only dried mushrooms crumble.

Oven

Drying mushrooms in the oven is very simple. The main thing is to adhere to the rules and anyone will succeed. In order for the drying to go right, you need to purchase or make your own lattice that would go into the oven. Lattices can be built from the ordinary wire.

Previously, the mushrooms are cleaned, and large ones are cut into several parts. Mushrooms are placed loosely on the wire rack; it is advisable to keep them a small distance apart. After we set the oven to a temperature of 45 °. In this mode, the stove should be turned on until its surface dries. After that, increase the temperature to 70-80 degrees and leave until you notice that they have completely dried up. Do not forget that small mushrooms dry faster. They can be pulled out, and the rest left to dry. Do not forget to occasionally swap the grilles so that the mushrooms are dried on all sides evenly.

It is important to leave the oven door ajar during drying - this will ensure air exchange.

Microwave

This device is in almost every home. With its help, you can quite tolerably dry your mushrooms. To do this, as always, we clean and cut the mushrooms, put in one layer on a plate and put in the microwave. We set the timer for 20 minutes. at a power of 100-180 watts, after which we open the oven, and allow moisture to weather. This usually takes 10-20 minutes. Then we repeat the same actions another 2-3 times. Not all microwaves can cope with some types of mushrooms, so sometimes they will need to be dried in some other way.

This method is more suitable for drying a small batch of mushrooms, otherwise, you will be doing this for more than one day. Not everyone has large microwaves at home, and not everyone has the patience to dry in a standard one, even for 2-3 lots.

Gas-burner

This is a fairly quick drying method, but it takes a long preparation to complete it. The method that we want to offer you was invented by engineer A. Lukyanov.

So, you need to take 4 cans, with a capacity of at least 5 kg. For three, trim the lids and the bottom; for the fourth, only the lid. The last can will be placed directly on the burner. In other banks, you need to make holes and insert needles into them. Mushrooms are strung on these knitting needles.

Next, put the jar with the bottom on the burner, and on top of it - all the other banks. During drying, banks will periodically need to be swapped.

Previously, a Russian oven was used to dry mushrooms. Now it's rare to find such units. Mushrooms were cooked directly in the oven on grills, wickers or knitting needles. They were loaded only when the oven cooled down a bit.

CHAPTER 13

Fascinating Facts About Magic Mushrooms And Magic Truffles

1. Magic Mushrooms and Magic Truffles Offer Some Incredible Benefits To Health

There is evidence that psychoactive compounds are a great alternative to standard treatment for mental health disorders in magic mushrooms and truffles, psilocybin and psilocyn. Therefore, it is understood that magic mushrooms do not cause physical dependence. Psilocybin and Psilocyn help to balance the amygdala (a group of nuclei involved in emotion processing) by altering the response of our brains to negative stimuli.

However, the active ingredients give an effective cure for migraine and cluster headaches. Patients with this sort of headache know how difficult it is to find a cure for it.

2. There Are Hundreds Of Various Species Of Psychedelic Mushrooms

There are about 200 different types of magic mushrooms and truffles. They grow in many different landscapes, from grasslands and gardens, over rotted forests, to animal manure.

3. The Use Of Magic Mushrooms Is As Old As Humanity Himself

The consumption of magic mushrooms and magic truffles did not start with the hippie movement in the 1970s, contrary to popular belief. He's actually going back a lot more. The Viking warriors were thought to use magic mushrooms before battle to get themselves into a trance-like state of anger.

In Central America, the Aztecs called magic mushrooms "the flesh of the gods" and often used them in religious ceremonies. In the Sahara, even statues and hieroglyphs were found with figures holding large mushroom-like objects in their hands.

4. Magic Mushrooms And Truffles Can Positively Change Your Personality

Research by the University of Medicine Johns Hopkins in 2011 found that people reported increasing general well-being after taking psilocybin once a day for at least the next 14 months. The personality change involves impartiality, self-confidence, satisfaction, and optimism.

Being able to enhance personality after the age of 25 is very rare for an active ingredient. This is possible because customers identify their magic mushroom experience as one of their life's five greatest spiritual experiences.

5. Magic Mushrooms And Truffles Promote The Growth Of New Brain Cells

Tests have shown that even small doses of psilocybin can boost the regeneration of brain cells and help repair damaged cells in the brain. This process is known as neurogenesis. Scientists are exploring the possibility of curing Alzheimer's using magic mushrooms.

6. Animals Also Rely On Magic Mushrooms

According to a BBC nature documentary from 2009, Siberian reindeer have a weakness for magic mushrooms and magic truffles. It is not certain if they have a hallucinogenic effect, but they are not the only animals with a craving for the mystical fungus. Goats and other animals allegedly also consume magic mushrooms.

7. Magic Mushrooms Might Have Played A Role In The Evolution Of Humans

Controversial is the Theory of "The Stoned Ape Theory," founded by writer and psychonaut Terence McKenna. This notes that in advanced human evolution, hallucinogenic mushrooms have played a crucial role. McKenna claims that the effects of psilocybin have helped people to sharpen their gaze, making them better hunters in turn. Because they serve as natural aphrodisiacs, he also notes that magic mushrooms promote human reproduction.

8. In Some Countries In The Middle East Halluzinogene Fungi Is Completely Legal

Most Middle East countries are known to be highly conservative, punishing alcohol and other drugs harshly. In this part of the world, however, magic mushrooms are approved. There are areas where magic mushrooms are sold and eaten freely in some countries, such as Bali, and that's 100% legal!

9. Magic Mushrooms And Truffles Can Help In Various Dependencies

Magic truffles and magic mushrooms are an effective weapon in the battle against common dependencies, especially alcohol and tobacco. After a religious mushroom trip, customers say that they are confused about why they take harmful substances and eventually it inspires them to give up this habit.

10. Possession And Cultivation Of Magic Mushrooms Is Permitted Only In Two European Countries

Cultivation and possession of magic mushrooms are absolutely legal in the Czech Republic and Spain. This makes them the only countries in Europe where this is allowed. However, thanks to various loopholes, inhabitants can possess magic truffles and mushroom spores.

Good Tips for Great Trips

A trip with psilocybin is not just a trip and may be a heavy experience for some people, so it is very important that you are well prepared, that you feel good and are in the right attitudes when you start a trip.

Here Some Tips For A Good Trip

You Must Feel When You Reply The Trip.

Make sure you are in the right mood and environment. Mushrooms are emotionally invigorating. If you are in a bad mood and do not feel well, you have a greater chance of a horror trip than if you have a good feeling.

Choose A Relaxed And Trustworthy Environment.

Make sure you have a relaxed and trusting environment with people you can trust. Especially during an intense trip to an unknown place with people you do not know, this is a good recipe for a horror trip and a bad experience. Trust us, a trip on a Saturday afternoon in a busy shopping center is not fun ...

Take Your Time

Take your time, even after your trip. A trip due to the mushrooms may be an intense experience. Therefore, taking your time is necessary. Before you start, prepare yourself mentally. And don't go on a trip with your mind full of things that happened during the day after a long day in the office. You should still have a quiet time even after the trip. The mind needs time to process the events on an intense trip. Planning a relaxing day with no responsibilities for the day after the trip is always safer so that you can focus on what's going on during the trip.

Take Magical Truffle On Empty Stomach.

When you do this, the body absorbs psilocybin quicker, reducing the likelihood of vomiting at the start of the trip. As a rule, between the last meal and the intake of the magic truffle should always be a minimum of 3 hours. Ideally, during the day, it's good not to over-eat. And if you want to eat something good and easy to digest, that's what you want to do.

The Companion

A friend is a sober person who ensures that everything goes well and that people feel safe. It is definitely recommended to have a partner for beginners. A light snack should be offered before the trip: water, fruit juice, and herbal teas, as well as food. Magic truffles have an impact lasting 3 to 6 hours, so it is a relatively long time.

During this time, eating and drinking are often forgotten. This can be hard because during thid time you may not be hungry. Yet eating and drinking during this time make sense. It can be hard to find your way to the fridge during the trip, so it makes sense to have food and drink nearby.

Do Not Combine With Other Conscious Substances

Do not use magical truffles with other drugs that alter the mind. Psychedelics like psilocybin, like nothing else, plan an impression. Combining it with another drug that can have certain effects on the body and mind is not advised, as it can in many cases lead to a less pleasant experience. We only have one exception: marijuana. A bit of grass is very calming just before or at the end of the trip. It varies from individual to individual.

CONCLUSION

The unique effects produced by psilocybin provide panoramas for the study of the mind in general and human consciousness in particular. They allow the exploration of various parameters and mechanisms linked to the conscious process, such as sensory perception and self-awareness.

In the hands of the therapist, psilocybin cannot only act frankly on the resurgence of repressed memories, but also arouse a desire for rapprochement between the patient and the therapist, forming a bond where greater collaboration on both sides is possible to reveal the origin of mental disorders.

These mushrooms have shown themselves to be an effective therapeutic tool, and prove my hypothesis that the prohibition of this substance comes rather from a prejudiced arbitrariness of heinous grounds rather than it being a real risk to the life or welfare of the human being. However, for a safe and beneficial application of psilocybin as an auxiliary tool in therapeutic processes, further studies are needed.

Consumption of some mushrooms can cause stomach pain, diarrhea, nausea and vomiting. It can also make mental illness worse or even trigger it.

Another consequence of this drug could be accidents caused by misinterpretation of reality.

There are poisonous mushrooms that can be very toxic or even lethal. Amanita is a very dangerous drug and is currently responsible for 90% of fatal cases of fungal poisoning. Prolonged use of this species may lead to mental weakness. Excessive doses can cause delusions, seizures, deep coma and death due to cardiac arrest.

Made in the USA
Coppell, TX
17 February 2020